Volume 2

DRAMA

for

WORSHIP

Volume 2

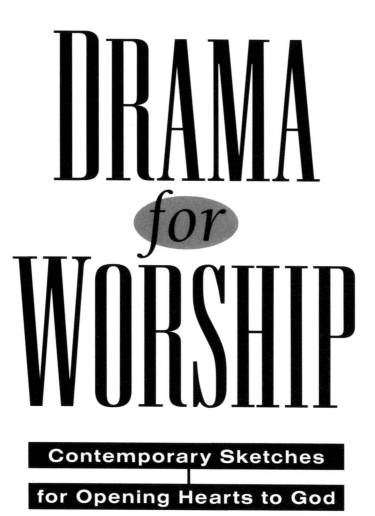

DRAMA *for* WORSHIP

Contemporary Sketches
for Opening Hearts to God

Curt Cloninger

Standard Publishing
Cincinnati, Ohio

Drama for Worship, Volume 2
© 1999 by Curt Cloninger
All rights reserved
ISBN 0-7847-0917-3

Designed by Steve Diggs and Friends
Edited by Lise Caldwell

The Standard Publishing Company, Cincinnati, Ohio
A division of Standex International Corporation
Printed in the United States of America

06 05 04 03 02 01 00 99   5 4 3 2 1

Library of Congress Cataloging-in-Publication Data

Cloninger, Curt.
    Drama for worship / Curt Cloninger.
            p. cm.
    Contents: v. 1. 8 sketches and monologues — v. 2. 8 sketches and monologues.
    ISBN 0-7847-0916-5
    1. Drama in public worship.   2. Christian drama, American.
    I. Title.
BV289.C57   1999   98-44071
246'.72—dc21

For Tish and Kap and Lily

Contents

How to Use This Hammer

They should come with warning labels; hammers, saws and the like. "Caution: In the right hands, this hammer will prove extremely effective for many household projects. In the wrong hands, someone could lose a thumb." Some folks are great with household implements. Not me. More than once, I've come close to losing a thumb. But, I've got this friend, Mark, who's a whiz with tools. So, usually, when I'm faced with a major household project, I give Mark a call and he comes right over, tools in hand. He swiftly (and painlessly) cuts the needed trim work or patches the gaping Sheetrock hole. I stand and watch in amazement. When Mark's done, I thank him profusely and he mumbles a reply. Something like, "Aww, it's nothing. You just gotta have the right tools and know how to use 'em." Exactly. That's why I give Mark a call in the first place. He's got the right tools and he knows how to use 'em.

So, you're doing theater in your church. You're maybe in the "banging your thumb" stage, or maybe you're already doing some incredible handiwork. But, there's one thing for sure; whether you're just getting started with church drama, or whether you're a seasoned theater veteran, it always helps to have the right tools. I've learned that one of the foundational tools in any theater situation is a good script. Hopefully, this book will provide you with that tool.

This book is full of what I like to call "Good Used Scripts." These scripts have been around the block a time or two. They've been tested, critiqued, and picked over, by actors in the rehearsal process, by pastors in the theological review process, and by my wife in the "Does this ring true to life?" process. The scripts are born out of my ministry at Perimeter Church, where I've been on part-time staff since 1994 as a sort of "Artist-in-Residence." We do a lot of theater at Perimeter Church. We need lots of scripts. Because of my years of training in theater, I've become the "Designated Writer" there, but I'm also an actor. Since 1982 my full-time job has been as a professional actor, traveling and performing solo theater all over North America. In my travels, I'm in churches with many different styles, including contemporary, traditional, and "seeker-sensitive." And I hear a lot of pleas for scripts. That's why I've finally published some of the things I've written for Perimeter.

You'll notice that there's a wide variety of topics represented here. Most of the scripts can be performed with minimal props and sets, and with few actors. (I know what it's like trying to round up and rehearse too many busy people!) Some of these scripts aim to just "set the table." That is, they will simply introduce a topic, but not attempt to answer too many questions. Some of them, however, attempt to give specific theological answers to real-life questions. Some will work best when combined with sermons or songs. Some work best standing entirely on their own. You'll also notice that I don't shy away from gritty life issues. I'm a firm believer that the grace of God, as evidenced in Jesus, is the ultimate response to this grit.

I hope you are stretched by the performing or even by the reading of these scripts. I hope that in performing them, you'll help open peoples' minds, but, even more importantly (for this is the strong suit of theater), that you'll help open peoples' hearts to the good news of the scandalous love of God for his people. I hope you create some incredible handiwork. You'll probably bang a few thumbs. That's just part of the process and quite to be expected. God bless you as you build!

Curt Cloninger

For more information on Curt Cloninger's solo work, check out his web page at *www.curtcloninger.com*.

Fish Story

Synopsis:
Joe, Andy, and Jenny are in a fishing contest. Joe becomes frustrated by his daughter's ability to catch fish by color-coordinating the lures with her outfit. Andy reminds Joe that all of them will win the prize based on Jenny's catch of fish. Joe winds up with the most unusual catch of all.

Scriptural background:
Romans 5, 6

Suggested topics:
Grace, imputed righteousness, acceptance of Christ's sacrifice

Characters:
Joe, a recreational fisherman
Andy, Joe's brother
Jenny, Joe's teenage daughter

Props:
- boat
- three fishing poles
- brightly-colored lures, one still in its original box
- tackle box
- 6 "fish," 5 of which are on a stringer
- can of Coca-Cola soft drink
- Walkman portable radio
- old boot
- blue chiffon or cardboard "waves" to mask the "fishing"

Setting:
A fishing boat on a lake during a fishing contest

Joe, Andy, *and* Jenny, *are in a fishing boat. All three have their poles in the water downstage of the boat. As the action begins,* Jenny *is pulling in a big bass.* Joe *reacts with chagrin.* Andy *is laughing.*

Jen: All right!! I got another one! [*as she pulls it in*] Daddy, will you please get this one off too? I really hate to feel their slimy little mouths.

Joe: [*perturbed*] No. I will not get this one off. I got the last eleven off. You would think that if a girl can catch twelve fish she could at least take them off the hook. I refuse. It's your turn.

Jen: Well, you don't have to get all huffy about it. Uncle Andy, will you take it off? Pleeeeze?

Andy: [*laughs*] Sure, Jen. Pass it over here. [*takes the fish off the hook, holds it up and looks at it, then puts it in the well*] Hey, I think this might be the biggest one you've caught all day. [*to* Joe] Joe, you oughta be glad Mary made us take her with us. She keeps catching them like this and we're a shoo-in to win this thing. [*stage whisper to* Jen, *but still able to be heard by* Joe] And don't you worry about your Dad, honey. He's just having to deal with a little "angler envy," that's all.

Joe: I heard that. I'm not having "angler envy." I'm just—curious.

Jen: [*innocent*] Curious? About what, Daddy?

Joe: About how a girl who's never been fishing could catch every fish of the day. And me, the expert, not two feet away from her, and I catch nothing. Nada. Zippo.

Jen: Oh, that's easy, Daddy. I pick the little dangly thingys [*referring to the lures*] to match my outfit. I think it helps to have everything color-coordinated. [*holds a lure up next to her earrings*] Like this one. See how good this looks right next to my earrings? Oooh! In fact, these would be great earrings!

Andy: [*still amused*] You're right, Jen. Perfect match. [*to* Joe] I think she's got something here, Joe. [*holding up a lure*] If I were you, Joe, I'd use one of these little green thingamajigs. It picks up the highlights in your eyes very nicely. Quite stunning.

Joe: Very funny. It's just a little humiliating to be outfished by a total novice.

Andy: Hey, Joe, look on the bright side. If she keeps catching fish like this one, we're gonna win this fishing tournament, hands down.

Joe: Who says?

Jen: You said, Dad.

Andy: She's right, Joe. You did say that this thing is judged by the ten best fish per boat, not per person.

Jen: Yeah, Dad. You said it didn't matter who caught the fish.

Joe: Well, that's when I thought I'd be the one catching the fish. [*sulking*] It's just not fair, that's all.

Andy: You're right, Joe. It's not fair. I say we just dump all twelve of the fish Jen caught back in the lake. Let's forget the thousand dollar first prize we'd probably win and just dump all thirty pounds of these fish right back into the water [*starts for the well*].

Joe: [*quickly moves to stop* Andy] Now wait a minute! Let's not do anything rash here! After all, rules are rules. [*hesitantly*] And the rules do say that we get credited for what she catches. Right?

Andy: Works for me.

Joe: [*trying to convince himself*] So, all we have to do is just accept it, right?

Andy: That's right, Joe. We must accept the fact that we're gonna win a thousand bucks based on the catch of a close to novice teenage girl who catches fish by color-coordinating her thingamajig with her earrings.

Joe: [*still trying to convince himself, and continuing to fish*] Yeah—we've just gotta accept it and keep fishing.

Andy: Well, actually Joe, I don't think we need to keep fishing. We can win this thing based on Jen's ten best fish. She's got quite a haul there. I mean, we can't do any better than what she's already done. I say we just kick back, break out the sandwiches and have a Coke. [*to* Jen] Hey, Jen, pass me a drink there, will ya?

[Jen *gets a Coca-Cola out of the cooler and hands it to* Andy. *He opens it, takes a sip, and sits back. During this whole conversation* Jen *is trying out lures, holding them up to her outfit, etc., and listening to her Walkman radio, bopping to the music. Andy is kicked back, and Joe is furiously changing lures.*]

Andy: [*casually*] This is great. You know, this whole thing sorta reminds me of something I studied in that Bible course I took.

Joe: Andy, don't start with the Bible course stuff again. I don't wanna hear it! You're boring me to tears! And why in the world did you take a Bible Correspondence Course?! Why didn't you take something practical, like tax preparation or . . . taxidermy.

Andy: [*laughs*] That'd be great. Then I could mount all the fish you didn't catch. I don't know why I took a Bible course. It just seemed like a good idea at the time. Anyway, this whole thing: Jen catching the fish, but you and me getting the credit, is a lot like what they called in my class, "imputed righteousness."

Joe: Right. "Reputed righteousness." And now you're gonna tell me the story of Noah and the whale. [*to Jen who does not hear a word he's saying because she's listening to music through her headphones*] You remember I told you that story, honey, about Noah and the whale—how he got all those animals and then a whale swallowed them all.

Jen: [*shouting*] What, Dad?

Joe: Nothing.

Andy: [*gets more and more excited as he gets into this illustration*] Joe, it's Jonah and the whale. And it's not "reputed." It's "imputed." "Imputed righteousness." Now, do you wanna hear this or not.

Joe: Yeah, sure.

Andy: Okay. This is how it works. God is perfect, right? Okay, we'll call perfect five fish [*holds up the stringer of fish*].

Joe: Put the fish down, Andy.

Andy: But, we are not perfect. We're not even close to perfect. We'll call that, uh, no fish. Kinda like you, Joe. Now, here's the scary part. The only way to be with God is to be perfect. Five fish. Uh, oh, we've got a problem here. We got no fish. Zero. In fact, we don't have a boat—we don't even have poles. Now, here's the neat part. Jesus is perfect. Five fish. And, he's got a great boat. This is so great! If we will get in the boat with Jesus, perfection, five fish, then we get credited with perfection because we're in the boat with Jesus. And all we've gotta do is trade in our non-perfection for it and accept it. We just gotta get in the boat. Neat, eh?

Joe: I don't believe that "imputed whatever." It couldn't be that simple. "Get in the boat with Jesus." Look, I believe that if you wanna deal with God, you've gotta bring something to the table. I mean, "God helps those who help themselves." That's in the Bible, right?

Andy: Oh, yeah. It's right next to the verses that say, "Cleanliness is next to godliness" and "Don't go swimming for at least an hour after you eat."

Joe: Well, anyway, that's what I believe. I believe there's no free lunch.

Andy: Yeah, and look what that's got you.

Joe: What?

Andy: No free lunch—and NO FISH!

Joe: I'll get fish. Just watch me. I've got my best jig on now.

He casts his line downstage of the boat. Someone should be hidden there in the "waves." This person will attach the shoe to Joe's *line and pull on the line where indicated.*

Andy: Well, I hope your fishing turns out better than your theology.

Joe: My theology's just fine, thank you. [*muttering to himself*] Imputed, reputed—whatever.

There is a humongous pull on Joe's *line.*

Jen: Ohhhhh, Daddy, you got something!

Joe: You bet I got something. Can you see it, Andy?

Andy: I don't know Joe, reel it in!

Joe: Is it a good one, Andy? Is it a bass?!

Andy: [*He and the audience know* Joe *has caught a shoe.* Joe *doesn't know yet.*] Ohhh, yeah, Joe, it's a Bass all right.

Joe: You bet it's a bass! And it's not just "imputed" either! [*to* Jen] Now, you just sit back, Jen, and I'll show you what a real contribution to the fish count looks like! How big is it, Andy? It feels like a ten pounder!

Andy: [*reading the inside of the loafer*] Oh, yeah, it's at least a ten.

Joe: You bet it's a ten! A ten pound bass!

Andy: Actually, Joe, it looks more like a twelve.

Joe *pulls up a large boot which is attached to his lure.*

Andy: A twelve triple E Bass Weejun! OOOOO! Joe! Nice one! Should we use that in our total weight count? Or maybe they have a category for footwear.

Joe: Give me a break, will ya?

Jen: [*Has been reading the fishing lure box that* Joe *has discarded after attaching the lure to his line. She shows* Joe *the box in which the lure came.*] Dad, of course you caught a shoe. Read the box. It says right here: "Good for catching sole."

Andy: Joe, maybe you better just get in the boat with Jesus.

Hat in Hand

Synopsis:

Ron and Chip were business partners until Chip swindled Ron out of $300,000. That was several years ago. Chip is now a Christian and has come to Ron to ask for forgiveness. Ron may not be ready.

Scriptural background:

Mark 11:25, Luke 17:3

Suggested topics:

Forgiveness, repentance, friendship, debt

Characters:

Ron, a family man in his thirties or forties
Chip, his old friend

Props:

- lawnmower
- baseball cap
- envelope

Setting:

Ron's front yard

Ron *is hunched over, fiddling with his lawnmower.* Chip *approaches and stands unnoticed for a moment, watching* Ron. *Then* Chip *hesitantly walks up and speaks.*

Chip: Hey.

Ron: [*doesn't look up, and continues to work on the mower*] Hey, yourself.

Chip: Having trouble with that thing?

Ron: Yeah, I—[*looks up and sees who is speaking to him; the sun is slightly in his eyes, so he shields them*] Chip?

Chip: Yeah . . . yeah . . . it's me.

Ron: [*stands up; uncomfortable pause*] Well . . .

Chip: It's been awhile.

Ron: A long while.

Chip: Yeah.

Ron: [*very uncomfortable*] So—you just passing through?

Chip: No, actually—I live here now.

Ron: Here?

Chip: Yeah. Here. In Atlanta.

Ron: Ah.

Chip: I've got an apartment—and a job as a programmer.

Ron: How long have you been here?

Chip: About six months now.

Ron: Oh.

Chip: It took me awhile to work up . . . to come here . . . to see you.

Ron: [*coolly*] Yeah.

Chip: I wasn't real sure what you would think of that. [Ron *just looks at* Chip] I wasn't real sure.

Ron: [*after a long pause*] Let me to make this easy for you, Chip. I've got a hat. [*takes off the baseball cap he's wearing and hands it to* Chip] Here. Now you can approach me with a hat in your hand. I'm afraid that's all I've got left to give you.

Chip: [*plunging ahead*] Ron, I need you to forgive me. *You* need you to forgive me.

Ron: [*incredulous*] Oh. I do?

Chip: Yeah.

Ron: [*angry*] And why is that, Chip?

Chip: Because I've got a gut full of remorse and you've got a gut full of bitterness, and neither one of us needs that in our gut. We're not getting—

Ron: [*dismissive*] Look. You swindled me out of three hundred thousand dollars. Remember? You should be in jail. I forgave you five years ago when I didn't press charges. So don't lecture me about forgiveness. You're scot-free. If that's not forgiveness, I don't know what is.

Chip: [*after a long pause, very tentatively*] Yeah . . . yeah. [*trying to change the subject*] You know how when we were in business together, you were always trying to get me to go to church with you. Well, I—

Ron: [*interrupting, scornful*] Don't tell me. You've had a jailhouse conversion, and you haven't even been to jail. If that's not just like you! Very convenient that you had this AFTER you took off with all our money.

Chip: I've never been one for timing.

Ron: I'd say your timing's pretty good.

Chip: [*trying to figure out how to approach this*] Ron, if somebody had asked me five years ago, I would've said that I wanted your forgiveness. But, I know now, I didn't.

Ron: [*angry*] Yeah.

Chip: I just didn't want to go to jail. But I didn't want forgiveness, so I didn't get it.

Ron: What's your point?

Chip: I want it, now, Ron. I'm asking for your forgiveness. I've hurt you, and your family.

Ron: You certainly have.

Chip: But it's more than that. I've sinned against you, your family, God. And I'm sorry, Ron. I really am. God's forgiven me. That's what I was gonna tell you.

Ron: [*not quite as cold*] Well, that's great.

Chip: But, Ron, you haven't forgiven me. Please forgive me. I want things to be right between us. I guess I've been praying that you might want the same thing.

Ron: [*after a pause*] I don't know, Chip. I don't know.

Chip: [*almost with hope*] The way I see it is, we both have something to swallow here.

Ron: And what's that?

Chip: Our pride. But that's a lot better than what's in our guts right now, huh?

Ron: [*pauses and looks at his watch, then turns his back on* Chip] Look, uh, Ginger's gonna be home with the kids in a few minutes. I don't really think she'll want to see you here.

Chip: No, I guess not. [*He makes an adjustment on the lawn mower, then starts it and quickly turns it off. Ron turns around quickly to see the started mower. Chip hands him an envelope.*] Here.

Ron: What's this?

Chip: It's my phone number. I'd love to get together with you—when you're ready. I'm serious. [*hesitates*] There's also a check in there.

Ron: A check?

Chip: Yeah.

Ron: I thought your gambling debts busted you.

Chip: Yeah, they did. But, you know me. I got a real creative lawyer, and he managed to let me keep my house. I just sold it. There was seventy thousand dollars in equity. [*indicating the envelope*] It's all there. [*almost with a chuckle*] A cashier's check. Only two hundred thirty thousand to go. [*forces a slight laugh, and gets no response from Ron*] I'll see you. [*turns and starts to walk off, then realizes that he still has Ron's baseball cap in his hands*] Oh. Here. Sorry.

Ron: [*unsure what to do, and says almost tenderly*] No. Keep the hat. [*after a pause*] Listen, I'll call you sometime.

I Do?

Synopsis:
Lisa and Brent rush to the courthouse to get married while their love is still "new." The Judge's unusual wedding ceremony forces them to reevaluate their readiness for lifelong commitment.

Scriptural background:
Genesis 2:23, 1 Corinthians 13:4-8

Suggested topics:
Marriage, commitment, infatuation versus love

Characters:
Lisa, the bride
Brent, the groom
Judge, old, gruff, and bit deaf, but very wise

Props:
- judge's robe
- papers
- judge's bench
- fifty dollar bill
- certificate
- telephone
- purse
- law book

Setting:
The Judge's courtroom

Lisa *and* Brent *tentatively approach the* Judge's *bench, seeking to be married.*

Judge: [*as he looks down at the paperwork on his desk*] All right, all right, what do we have here? Traffic accident?

Brent: [*nervously*] Uh, no, your Honor. We want to get married, Your Honor.

Judge: Married, is it? Well, why didn't you say so? [*muttering to himself*] Married—everybody wants to get married. [*to* Lisa] So, you wanna get married, eh?

Lisa: Yessir?

Judge: So, why are coming to me, instead of having a church wedding?

Brent: [*excited*] Oh, we couldn't wait, Your Honor.

Judge: For what?

Brent: To get married.

Judge: Oh. Right.

Brent: [*sickeningly sweet*] We're very much in love, Your Honor, and we can't wait for a church wedding.

Lisa: [*sickeningly sweet*] We want to start our life together. Right now. Today.

Brent: While we're at the peak of our compatibility.

Lisa: While the glow of love is still in the air.

Brent: While we're sure of our everlasting devotion to one another.

Lisa: While—

Judge: [*interrupting*] All right, I get the picture. You're . . . motivated.

Brent: Yessir!

Judge: Well, have you got everything you need?

Brent: Like what, Your Honor?

Judge: Well, to start with, fifty bucks and a blood test.

Lisa: [*pulls a fifty dollar bill and a blood test certification out of her purse*] Yes sir! Here's the money, and here's the result of our blood test. [*pointing out the paper*] I'm proud to say that even our blood types are completely compatible.

Judge: I'm thrilled.

Brent: So, uh, Your Honor, could we—uh—could we get on with it?

Judge: You want to "Get on with it"? All right! [*deciding to "lay it on heavy"*] Repeat after me: I, Brent, take you, Lisa, to be my lawfully wedded wife.

Brent: I, Brent, take you, Lisa, to be my lawfully wedded wife.

Judge: To have and to hold from this day forward,

Brent: To have and to hold from this day forward,

Judge: As long as we both shall live.

Brent: As long as we both shall live.

Judge: Okay, Lisa. The same goes for you. Do you?

Lisa: I do.

Brent: Great! That's it, huh? [*leaning in to kiss Lisa*] Now, do we do the kiss thing?

Judge: Not so fast there, bucko! We've got more.

Brent: There's more?

Judge: In my court, there is. Now, you both just say "I do" or "Yessir" when I ask you these questions.

Lisa & Brent: Yessir.

Judge: [*gives them a wilting look*] Wait 'til I ask the question. Let's see here. [*flipping through his book*] Brent, you're gonna marry this woman for life, right?

Brent: Yessir!

Judge: So, do you promise to love her even when you don't feel like it?

Brent: [*unsure how to answer*] I do?

Judge: Even when she doesn't look as good as she does right now?

Brent: Excuse me?

Judge: Even six months after the birth of your third child when she hasn't taken off those extra thirty-five pounds?

Brent: What?

Judge: [*getting wound up*] Are you gonna respect her even when she refuses to get up in the middle of the night to clean up the throw-up from your six year old because she says it's your turn to clean up the throw-up because she cleaned it up the last eight times in a row?

Brent: Huh?

Judge: Do you promise to be all ears and make a big deal out of it when she's telling you some long boring story about some obscure girlfriend of hers, BUT NOT to make a big deal out of it when she backs your '87 Dodge Caravan into a new Lexus in the grocery store parking lot?

Brent: Sir, I'm.not sure I'm understanding—

Judge: All right, how about this one? Do you, Brent, promise to stick with this woman even when she really, really ticks you off, and what you'd really like to do is, at best, humiliate her in public, and at worst, haul her down to some divorce court in Las Vegas?

Brent: [*shocked*] Huh?

Judge: Okay. Now, Lisa—it's your turn.

Lisa: [*weakly*] Yessir?

Judge: Do you, Lisa, promise to love this man even when he's old and fat and has long since quit trimming his nose hairs?

Lisa: Sir?!

Judge: Do you promise not to roll your eyes when he recounts, for the two hundredth time, in nauseating detail, how he almost eagled that par five six years ago?

Lisa: But, he doesn't even play—

Judge: Do you promise to respect him when he fusses at you for not buying generic dishwashing soap, while he himself buys a new piece of stereo equipment every time the moon is full?!

Lisa: Well, I—

Judge: Do you promise to honor him, even when it becomes apparent to you and to all your girlfriends, that you're a whole lot smarter than he is?

Lisa: I—

Judge: And finally, do you promise to stick with this man even when he really, really ticks you off, and you'd like to, at best, abandon him in some mine shaft in Arizona and, at worst, arrange for your cousin Butch to rearrange his face a little?

Brent *and* Lisa *just look at each other in shock, unable to respond.*

Brent: [*finally stammers out*] Sir, could we just have a minute?

Judge: You don't have a minute. You want to get married, right? Well, this all goes with the territory. Now, you can kiss each other. And then I'll make THE PRONOUNCEMENT.

Lisa: THE PRONOUNCEMENT?!

Judge: Yeah. The "Husband and Wife Forever and Ever Amen" part. [Brent *and* Lisa *look at each other, immobilized*] Now, this'll be your first kiss as a married couple. The first kiss of about ten jillion kisses, some of 'em pretty good, but a whole lot of 'em accompanied by bad breath or screaming kids. Your first kiss as a married couple, and from now on, for ever and ever amen, you won't kiss anybody else, not even so much as a peck on the cheek, for ever and ever amen, or until one of you KEELS OVER AND DIES!

Brent *and* Lisa *hesitate. They look at each other in horror. Then they look to the* Judge.

Judge: Well, what's the matter? Let's get on with it here! Kiss each other and I'll pronounce you—

Brent: [*interrupting*] NO! Don't pronounce us anything!

Lisa: We don't want to be pronounced! Please, DON'T PRONOUNCE US!

Judge: Don't pronounce you, huh? All right! then. I guess you two can go.

Lisa: [*They start to leave. Lisa turns tentatively*] What about our fifty dollars?

Judge: Nonrefundable.

Brent: No problem! Really. No problem. It's fifty dollars well spent.

The Judge watches Brent and Lisa quickly walk off in opposite directions. The Judge dials a number on the phone.

Judge: [*suddenly very sweet and charming*] Hello, dear? I was wondering if you'd like to have lunch today? [*listening*] Great! Bring the grand-kids. 12:30 at Café Amor. I've just come into a fifty dollar wind-fall. Cold feet . . . once again.

An Affair to Forget

Synopsis:

Jake describes how he allowed himself to be entangled in several "affairs." Only when he reveals that his "lovers" were credit cards do we see the lure and danger of such debt. This scene works best when the actor keeps his real secret from the audience as long as possible.

Scriptural background:

1 John 2:15, Romans 13:8

Suggested topics:

Debt, priorities, obedience to Jesus

Character:

Jake, a man recovering from several "affairs"

Props:

None

Setting:

Anywhere

Jake stands center stage. This monologue is his "confession."

Jake: She was beautiful. Small—petite would be a better word for her, I guess. Petite. My Golden Girl, I called her. Beautiful. I remember when I first met her. It was at the Post Office, strangely enough. I knew who she was. Everybody did. I never dreamed she'd ever have anything to do with me. She was pretty high class. I was sure she was way out of my league. But, she let it be known, in no uncertain terms, that she was interested in me. And, I'll tell you something: I was definitely interested in her.

Look. I know what some of you are thinking. And you're right. I was already in a relationship. And it *did* mean something to me. And I'm not a philanderer. At least, I didn't think of myself that way. I didn't go looking for trouble. But trouble just seemed to find me. It started out really innocently. I took her to lunch. I had a great time. Probably spent more than I should have, but I had a great time. Before long, I was taking her to lunch a lot. Then dinner. Then on little . . . shopping sprees. Then on BIG shopping sprees. It was getting way out of hand. She was with me all the time. She made me feel . . . special. Proud. She made me feel—well, I guess this sounds like a forty-something year old guy in a mid-life crisis—but, she made me feel *fulfilled*. Like I'm standing on the deck of the Titanic, holding her, shouting into the wind, "I'm the king of the world." My Golden Girl. Always at my side. I loved—well, I loved what she did for me.

I didn't even realize when things began to turn sour. She changed. She started demanding more and more from me. She told me I wasn't paying her enough interest. That I was just using her. But the funny thing was, I felt the same way. Like she was just using me. Getting all she could get from me. I know I should've just ended it. It's like I was drowning. I couldn't think straight. But it was like I had to have her just to get by. And that's when things began to get really desperate. One day she and I were on the outs. And that day, I met another one. And she was, well, incredible. A platinum. I know, I don't look like the platinum type. But she was a *real* platinum. And for awhile, a few months, I got the same old feeling. Like all of life was in my hip pocket. But then she started pushing. And demanding. And I was drowning even worse. Before long I was playing the two of 'em against each other, just to get some relief. But, it didn't work. I couldn't satisfy either one of 'em, and looking back on it now, I realize they couldn't satisfy me. Look, I'm ashamed to say this, but I brought another one into the whole affair. And this one—well, I was sure she was different. She seemed wholesome. American. And she *expressly* promised me that she only wanted what was best for me. That was a lie. She demanded, just like the other two. More and more interest. More and more time. It was killing me. Literally. I mean, my heart hurt.

Finally, one night, it all came crashing down around my head. That night I was rejected by all three of 'em. I couldn't sleep. I had no hope. I crawled back to my first love with my heart in my hands. I sat on the doorstep and I fessed up. I said, "I've been unfaithful. I've been running around, chasing others like a fool. And I'm sorry. Will you please forgive me?

And Jesus said, "Of course I forgive you. Now, listen. You cut up your gold and your platinum cards, and you follow me. I'm all you need."

I couldn't believe it. I said, "Are you sure?"

And he said, "Yeah, I'm sure."

And I said, "But, Jesus, what about the American Express?"

He thought for a minute. Then he said, "Do you love it?"

And I said, "No. Not really."

And he said, "Then keep it, for now. I may want you to buy me lunch some day."

And that was the end of that story and the beginning of many more.

Beyond Justice

Synopsis:
Jim comes home to find Erin preparing to leave him. She has been unfaithful, and her guilt overwhelms her. Jim forgives her, but she still wants to leave. Jim agrees to let her go, but only if he can go with her.

Scriptural background:
Proverbs 3:3, Luke 6:36

Suggested topics:
The mercy of God and how it affects the way we love others; marriage, forgiveness

Characters:
Erin, a wife who has been unfaithful
Jim, her husband

Prop:
Suitcase

Setting:
Living room or front hallway of a house

Jim *rushes in the door of his home to discover* Erin *about to leave, with a suitcase in her hand.*

Jim: I got your note.

Erin: Yeah, I thought you'd find it when you got back to the office from lunch. I didn't expect you'd come home, though.

Jim: Well, I did. Look, Erin, I think I know why you're doing this—

Erin: [*interrupting*] No, you don't. I can't stay here.

Jim: Yes! You can! You can stay here!

Erin: [*interrupting*] Jim, we don't need to talk about this anymore. I'm leaving. I don't think it would be right for me to stay. I'll just go away. You're an attorney. You can draw up the papers. I'll send you my address when I settle somewhere. I won't contest anything. You send me the papers, I'll sign them, and that will be that. A good clean break.

Jim: Erin, look! I'm not mad anymore! [*catches himself*] That's not true. I'm not *as* mad anymore. When I first found out, I wanted to kill the guy. I wanted to— [*catches himself*] But, it's not like that, now. I'm still hurt. I'd be lying if I told you differently. But I'm not so mad. I guess God just kinda took a lot of that out of me. I've thought about everything. I've looked at every scenario, and I want you to—

Erin: Jim, don't you get it? It's not just between you and me anymore! I've shamed you in front of everybody: all your colleagues, the church, your family. You don't need me here shaming you anymore.

Jim: Would you listen to me?! You messed up, Erin! You messed up. But, it's over, Erin. It's over! I don't want you to leave.

Erin: Yes, you do. Trust me, you do. You've got every right to hate me.

Jim: I don't hate you.

Erin: Well, you should. You should. You're making a big mistake. I've made mine, in spades. And if you don't hate me, you're making a big mistake.

Jim: I don't hate you, and I don't want you to leave.

Erin: Trust me. You do.

Jim: No, I don't! Erin . . . the worst of this is over, isn't it?

Erin: [*slow to come out of her mouth*] No, the worst is not over.

Jim: [*he knows*] What?

Erin: I'm—I'm—

Jim: [*finishes her sentence*] Pregnant. You're pregnant.

Erin: Yeah. I'm pregnant. I found out this morning.

Jim: [*almost to himself*] I've thought of this.

Erin: [*after a pause*] Everybody's worst nightmare has come true. And there's really nothing more to say, is there? Look, I can't stay here. I'm gonna go off and find a job somewhere. I'm gonna have this baby, then I'll place it for adoption, I guess. I don't expect you to support me. I don't expect anything from you. I'm getting just what I deserve. You know the law. You know that.

Jim: Erin, I—

Erin: [*interrupting, just trying to get through this*] I'm, uh, I'm just taking my clothes. They're all packed in my old car. I'm taking that too, if you don't mind. And I'm taking five thousand dollars that was in the household account. I'll leave everything else.

Jim: [*after a pause, slowly*] One question: Do you love me? Do you still care about me?

Erin: Yes. Don't you get it? That's why I'm leaving. I don't wanna put you through this.

Jim: [*pause*] Did you leave me a suitcase?

Erin: Yes—why?

Jim: [*pause*] Because I'd like to go with you.

Erin: What?

Jim: I'm gonna go with you, if you don't mind.

Erin: Go—go with me?

Jim: I'd like to stay married to you. And I'd like to go with you, wherever you're going. I'd like to—to make this work.

Erin: What about this baby?

Jim: [*after a beat*] Our baby? Is that who you're talking about? Our baby? I think this is gonna be one terrific kid.

Erin: Are you sure about this?

Jim: [*with tenderness*] I'll pack my suitcase.

Leaky Cups

Synopsis:

Two women, dressed in workout clothes, and with towels draped around their necks, talk about their lives. As they talk, they pour water from Evian bottles into the cups they are holding. The cups have holes in them, and the water pours from them as from a sieve. Soon we realize that their efforts to fill their lives are as futile as their efforts to fill their cups.

Scriptural background:

John 4:1-26

Suggested topics:

Fulfillment, peace, satisfaction

Characters:

One, a single career woman
Two, a married career woman

Props:

- two Evian natural spring water bottles
- two cups with small holes in the bottom
- two towels
- big "diamond" ring
- car keys
- two gym bags
- cross necklace

Setting:

Health club. You may wish to "scatter" towels on the floor to catch the water.

One and Two have just finished a workout. They are tired and out of breath.

Two: Good workout?

One: Great! You?

Two: Fantastic. Worn out.

One: Me too. Heart rate?

Two: Right where it should be.

One: Mine too.

Two: Great! [*referring to her body*] This is all we've got.

One: Gotta treat it right.

Two: Yep. Make it last.

One: Keep it young.

Two: Thirsty?

One: Dying. You?

Two: Yeah.

One: [*referring to water*] Evian?

Two: Yep. You?

One: [*laughs*] What else?

They both pour water. It leaks out. They don't even notice.

One: [*sees* Two's *keys in her bag or hand*] New car?

Two: Huh? Oh, yeah.

One: Lexus?

Two: Yes.

One: Nice looking cars. Dual airbags?

Two: Oh sure. Very safe. Really solid—last forever.

One: That's important.

Two: You bet.

Pause.

One: Thirsty?

Two: Can't get enough.

One: Me neither.

They both pour water. It leaks out. They sense something is wrong.

Pause.

One: How's work?

Two: Great! Busy. Yours?

One: Great! Got a promotion.

Two: No kidding?! How is it?

One: Great! [*more honest*] More stress.

Two: Of course. More challenge?

One: Oh yes.

Two: Good. More fulfillment?

One: [*hesitant*] Of course.

Two: [*pause*] Thirsty?

One: [*somewhat pensive*] Thirsty? Way thirsty.

Two: Me too. Never goes away.

They pour water. It leaks out. They pour more. It leaks out. They look at their Evian bottles.

Pause, then One *sees new ring on* Two's *finger.*

One: New ring?

Two: [*not impressed with the ring, because she knows what's behind it*] Yes.

One: From your husband?

Two: Mmm-hmmm.

One: [*pause*] Must be nice.

Two: [*slow to respond, then halfway honest*] It's . . . a marriage.

One: [*pause*] You love him?

Two: [*a bit of a cover, giving the "right answer"*] Sure.

One: He love you?

Two: Of course.

One: That's enough.

Two: [*pause, not sure*] Sure.

One: [*changing the subject*] Thirsty?

Two: Always.

One: [*a bit wistful, wishing there were more*] Yeah.

They pour the water into their cups. It leaks out. They become more and more uneasy.

Two: [*noticing a cross on a necklace around* One's *neck, she touches the necklace*] Nice cross. Are you religious?

One: Oh yeah.

Two: Go to church?

One: Sure.

Two: You like it?

One: Of course.

Two: What do you do?

One: At church?

Two: Yeah.

One: [*thinking*] Stay busy.

Two: At church?

One: Oh yeah.

Two: With what?

One: Groups, studies, programs, you know—stuff.

Two: [*wondering if this may be the answer*] It help?

One: With what?

Two: [*referring to their ever empty cups, their thirst*] You know.

One: [*knowing that it really doesn't help*] I guess.

Two: [*thinking about her thirst being satisfied*] That'd be nice.

One: [*wistful*] Yeah.

Pause. They both glance at their cups, almost not daring to look at them.

**One &
Two:** Thirsty?

**One &
Two:** Dying.

They both pour water into the cups. The cups leak. The lights fade.

Where Safe Is

Synopsis:

Liz meets her brother Terry at the airport. Terry asks Liz about the church she's going to. He wonders if church might be a safe place for him. Liz tells him that he doesn't have to wait until he's "fixed up" to come to church; he can come just as he is. This sketch works especially well when followed by the Sandy Patti song "Safe Harbour."

Scriptural background:

Hebrews 5:2, 2 Corinthians 1:3-6, Matthew 11:28-30

Suggested topics:

Sharing and showing God's love, church as a "safe place," dealing with homosexuality

Characters:

Liz, an outgoing southern gal
Terry, her brother
Flight Announcer

Props:

- row of chairs that resemble seats at an airport gate
- *Gentleman's Quarterly* magazine

Setting:

Delta gate in an airport terminal

As the scene opens we see Terry *sitting alone on a row of airport seats, reading a* GQ *magazine. We hear this announcement over the speakers: "Ladies and gentleman, we're beginning our initial boarding of Delta's flight 827 to Houston. Anyone needing a little extra time in the boarding process, please proceed now to gate 27."* Terry *looks at his watch and looks around, as if waiting for someone. Finally he spots his older sister* Liz, *hurrying down the corridor.* Liz *is VERY Southern.*

Terry: [*rising as he sees* Liz, *and warmly greeting her*] Hey, Sis. I thought I was going to miss you.

Liz: Hey, baby! I'm sorry I am late. The traffic was awful and I had trouble getting a parking spot. [*giving him a hug*] It's good to see you. It's been awhile.

Terry: Yeah.

Liz: So, where are you off to?

Terry: On my way home, actually. I've been in the Keys for a few days.

Liz: The life you lead! Well, this time at least you gave me a call.

Terry: You know how it goes. I guess I always figure it's not worth your while to drive all the way down to the airport just to see me for a few minutes.

Liz: Baby, it's worth my while. Trust me. I bet I haven't seen you in five years.

Terry: At least that.

Liz: If you gave me some advance notice when you're flying through, I'd bring Mom down to the airport to have a cup of coffee with you. She'd love that. She really misses seeing you, you know?

Terry: Yeah, yeah, I know that. Have you seen her lately?

Liz: Oh yeah. Last weekend. She came over and babysat the kids for the night while Greg and I went to Callaway Gardens.

Terry: She doing all right!?

Liz: [*laughs*] Oh yeah. Feisty as ever. So, how about you? You've lost some weight since last time I saw you.

Terry: I guess so.

Liz: [*checking out his tan*] You didn't get much sun in the Keys.

Terry: I'm not getting any younger. Gotta protect this old skin.

Liz: Tell me about it. So, how's your job?

Terry: Fine. It's fine. Same old job.

Liz: [*fishing*] And your love life? Any new girlfriends?

Terry: No, definitely not any girlfriends.

Liz: Well, baby, if you lived here I'd fix you up in a New York minute. All the single women I know would kill to meet somebody like you.

Terry: [*uncomfortable*] Yeah, well. Hey Sis, can I ask you something?

Liz: [*thinking she might have struck a chord*] Sure, baby.

Terry: Do you guys ever, ever go to church—you and Greg?

Liz: [*not understanding the sudden switch in topics*] Baby, where'd that come from?

Terry: I heard you were going to church.

Liz: Yeah, we've been going to church for about three years now. Who told you that?

Terry: Just some guy. It doesn't matter who. Do you go to Mamma's church?

Liz: No. No, we don't. Actually, Mamma doesn't even go to Mamma's church anymore. She's joined our church.

Terry: She left her old church?

Liz: Yeah.

Terry: I thought she was, like, one of the fixtures there.

Liz: [*laughs*] Well, fixtures move.

Terry: Why'd she leave?

Liz: She told me that her old church, how'd she put it, that they didn't seem to know what they believed anymore.

Terry: What's that mean?

Liz: She said her old church was so afraid of stepping on toes that they tiptoed around, never saying anything was wrong.

Terry: Like what?

Liz: [*avoiding the topic*] Oh, I don't know, just stuff.

Terry: What stuff?

Liz: [*hesitant to get into this*] Oh, I don't know. Like abortion or homosexuality or "shacking up," as Mamma says.

Terry: So your church is like, what, "hellfire and brimstone"?

Liz: [*laughs*] Hardly. Or me and Greg wouldn't be there.

Terry: [*trying to figure this out*] I thought you quit church a long time ago.

Liz: I did. About the same time you did. When I was old enough to leave home. Why are you asking me this, baby?

Terry: [*avoiding*] I was just wondering, that's all.

Liz: Wondering?

Terry: Yeah. Wondering. I haven't been to a church since, I don't know, I guess, tenth grade. And I was just wondering what church was like these days. If maybe a church might be a safe place for, [*alluding to his secret*] you know. [*obvious change of subject*] So, how are the kids.

Liz: [*answers quickly*] They're fine. [*pauses, then is ready to tackle the subject*] Terry, baby, I'm going to tell you something and I want you to just listen real close. Okay?

Terry: Okay.

Liz: About four years ago Greg and I were going through hell. He was drinking like a fish and I—I was having an affair. [*reacting to his reaction*] Yeah. Your big sister. It was a big mess. Greg and I were right on the verge of calling it quits. But for some reason Greg thought we should go to a counselor, just as a "one last shot" sort of deal. And I agreed to it. Well, Greg found this counselor. Greg liked him because he was cheap, but it turns out he was a Christian. Anyway, long story short, through this counselor Greg and I both discovered the love of God.

Terry: The love of God?

Liz: Yeah. And it wasn't some sweetsy church thing like I remember from when we were kids. It wasn't wishy-washy. It was very specific, and very powerful. The grace of God.

Terry: I have no idea what you're talking about.

Liz: What I'm talking about is, I met Jesus. Jesus Christ. And he changed my life. I don't how to be any plainer about it than that.

Terry: So you got your act together, and then you started going to this "hellfire and brimstone" church.

Liz: [*strongly*] No! No. I was messed up and *then* I met Jesus. And I started going to this church, and I met a bunch of other people who are just as messed up as I am. I'm not quite as messed up as I used to be. Jesus is changing me. [*gently*] But, Terry, the love of God was there the whole time, even from the beginning. It never went away. I don't understand it. But, it's true. And the church didn't have—you know—a bouncer, to keep all the messed up people out. They told me the truth. They told me my life, but they didn't keep me out.

Terry: [*reflective*] They didn't?

Liz: No. It's a good place. [*she ventures "into the fray"*] Baby, I've got a couple more things I want to say to you. And I don't want you to answer me. Not yet. Okay?

Terry: Okay.

Liz: Terry, baby, I'm going to tell *you* the truth. And if I'm wrong you tell me. I'm gonna tell you your life. [*gently venturing in*] I think I've known for a few years now that you're gay. I've never said anything because I didn't know what to say. You're a homosexual. I don't know why you are, or what makes you that way. But you are. And you fly off to Key West or to Provincetown or who knows where because you think that somehow, somewhere, with someone, you might find—what you're looking for. You might find where it's safe.

Terry: [*very touched, almost to himself*] Yeah.

Liz: And you fly through Atlanta, but you don't give me enough notice so I can meet you at the airport, because you're afraid. You're afraid I might find out about you. But, Terry, baby, I already know about you. And I've been praying for you. And you called today, Terry. You called today. Because you're not getting any younger. And you're not safe. But, you don't know where safe is, do you?

Terry: [*emotional, breaking down*] No, I don't. I don't. And I thought I didn't care. But I do care.

Liz: [*hugs him*] I can tell you where safe is, baby, 'cause I'm there. The only place where safe is: the love of Jesus.

At this point we hear an announcement for boarding: "Ladies and Gentlemen, we're now boarding Delta Flight 827 to Houston. We'll be boarding from the rear of the aircraft. Please, only board when your row number is called."

Liz: [*after listening to the announcement*] You could miss this flight, you know.

Terry: Yeah, I could.

Liz: You could come home with me. And I could cook dinner. And we could figure out where to go from here.

Terry: I'd like that.

Liz: So would I, baby. So would I.

One Small Spot

Synopsis:

Linda and Sam, two office workers, meet in the hall, waiting for the elevator to take them down to the lobby and home. They know each other well and enjoy bantering. When Linda notices that Sam is taking home some office supplies, Sam assures her that such theft is "only one small spot" on his record.

Scriptural background:

James 2:10

Suggested topic:

God's view of sin

Characters:

Linda, an office worker
Sam, her co-worker

Props:

- several boxes of paper clips
- fountain pen rigged to leak ink
- white shirt
- business card

Setting:

In front of the elevators in an office building

Linda *walks up to* Sam, *who is waiting for the elevator.* Sam *holds a couple of boxes of paper clips in his hands.*

Linda: Hey, Sam. How you doing? Hard day?

Sam: No more than usual, I guess. How about you?

Linda: Oh, not bad. I'm ready to get out of these heels, though. Whoever made the rule about women wearing heels to work oughta be shot.

Sam: [*chuckles as he loosens and takes off his tie*] I think it was the same guy who made up the rule about guys wearing ties and starched white shirts.

Linda: Yeah. [*notices the boxes of paper clips in* Sam's *hands*] What you got there?

Sam: Oh, just a couple of boxes of paper clips. I needed some at home.

Linda: [*curious*] You're taking boxes of office paper clips home?

Sam: [*not aware of the problem*] Yeah, sure. What's wrong with that? You got a problem with that? What, are you the "Paper Clip Sheriff" or something?

Linda: No! It's no skin off my nose. I've done the same thing myself. But, I've always felt kinda funny about it.

Sam: [*not believing her pickiness*] Linda, it's two boxes of paper clips, for Pete's sake! We're not talking grand theft larceny here!

Linda: [*chuckles*] Well, you know what they say, don't you? "Today, paper clips. Tomorrow, Fort Knox!"

Sam: Oh, give me a break! Are you telling me that taking home a couple of boxes of paper clips is the same thing as robbing Fort Knox?!

Linda: I don't know. I've always just felt funny taking home things from the office. You know, supplies and stuff. I've always had this feeling like God was leaning over some cloud somewhere with his radar gun on me. You know what I mean?

Sam: Linda, God doesn't care about a couple of boxes of paper clips! It's just not that big a deal in the cosmic scheme of things!

Linda: I guess you're right.

Sam: I mean, God may have his radar gun out, but he's not looking for me. I'm maybe going like one-tenth of a mile an hour over the speed limit. He doesn't care about that. God's looking for guys like Hitler, Saddam Hussein; you know, guys going about a zillion miles over the cosmic speed limit. He's not looking for perfection, you know what I mean?

Linda: I guess so. Still, I just always feel a little uneasy.

Sam: Linda. Come on! Lighten up! We're talking paper clips here! We're not talking "Major League Sin"! I'm an upstanding citizen, for Pete's sake. I'm a member of the Kiwanis Club. If taking home a box of paper clips puts some something on my record, it's just a little spot, that's all. Just one little spot! You're telling me that God's worried about one little spot?! Give me a break.

Linda: I guess you're right. Maybe I'm just a product of my repressive religious upbringing.

Sam: Well, you need to get free of that. I can give you the name of a great psychiatrist, if you want.

Linda: Sure, that'd be great. Why don't you write it down for me, or I'll forget it.

Sam: You got it. [*reaches into his pocket for a fountain pen*] His name is Dr. Borthwick. You got something I can write on?

Linda: Yeah, here [*hands him business card*].

Sam *begins to write down the name, but fumbles with the pen and paper clips. He winds up getting a large spot of ink on his perfectly white shirt.*

Sam: Oh great! I got ink on my shirt!

Linda: [*pulls out a handkerchief and hands it to* Sam] Here, why don't you see if you can get it off.

Sam: Forget it! It's ruined. A perfect, brand new, $75 Brooks Brothers shirt. This is the first time I've worn it!

Linda: Maybe your cleaners can get it out.

Sam: No way! This is india ink. This shirt is ruined.

Linda: [*drily*] That's a shame. 'Cause it's just one small spot.

About the Author

Curt Cloninger has loved theater for about as long as he has loved Jesus. Curt started acting in high school and hasn't quit yet. He received a B.A. in theater and communication from Abilene Christian University in 1976. He received further acting training at the Pacific Conservatory of the Performing Arts. Since 1982, Curt's full-time job has been as a solo performer. He has written many award-winning monologue theater pieces which he performs for conferences, churches, and colleges all over North America. He has performed in practically every denominational setting, and for audiences varying in size from 30 to 30,000.

Since 1994 Curt has served as an Artist-in-Residence with Perimeter Church, a large seeker-sensitive church in suburban Atlanta, Georgia. When Curt is not on the road performing his solo work, he is writing, directing, and performing in many of the theater pieces which Perimeter Church presents.

Curt has produced several award-winning videos, that have been used by thousands of people for curriculum and discussion starters. His current videos include "God-Views," "Witnesses," and "Red-Letter Edition."

Curt and his wife, Tish, have two children, Kap and Lily, and an assortment of critters (dogs, cats, fish and mice).

For more information on Curt Cloninger's solo work, or his videos, you may contact him at the address below:
P.O. Box 2353
Duluth, Georgia 30096
or
www.curtcloninger.com